The · Life Cycle · Series

The Life Cycle of a
WHALE

Bobbie Kalman and Karuna Thal
✿ Crabtree Publishing Company

www.crabtreebooks.com

The Life Cycle Series
A Bobbie Kalman Book

For my friends at The Unity Church of Hawaii
Dedicated by Karuna Thal
For my father, Stan Thal, who shared his love of the sea with me

Editor-in-Chief
Bobbie Kalman

Writing team
Bobbie Kalman
Karuna Thal

Editors
Niki Walker
Amanda Bishop
Kathryn Smithyman

Cover design
Campbell Creative Services

Computer design
Campbell Creative Services
Margaret Amy Reiach

Production coordinator
Heather Fitzpatrick

Photo research
Karuna Thal
Heather Fitzpatrick

Consultant
Patricia Loesche, Ph.D., Animal Behavior Program, Department of Psychology, University of Washington

Special thanks to: Lanny Sinkin, Dr. Marsha Green, Larry Morningstar, Ilona Selke, Michael Nolan, Robert Thomas, Roberta Goodman, Ginny Walden, Ron Piccari, and all the people who work to help keep our cetacean friends safe

Photographs
Frank S. Balthis: page 29
©Phillip Colla: pages 7 (bottom), 21, 25 (middle and bottom left);
    Photographs taken under provisions of NMFS Research Permit 882;
    title page, pages 23, 25 (top)
©Amos Nachoum/Seapics.com: page 9
©Michael S. Nolan/Wildlife Images: back cover (inset), pages 6, 12, 20, 22
©Doug Perrine/Hawaii Whale Research Foundation/Seapics.com: pages 13, 16
Tom Stack and Associates: Jeff Foott: page 5
©Masa Ushioda/Seapics.com: page 19
©K.A. Zirkle: page 18
Other images by Digital Stock

Illustrations
Barbara Bedell: page 5 (lower top right and bottom), 12
Patrick Ching: page 30 (middle)
Trevor Morgan: page 5 (upper top right)
Margaret Amy Reiach: series logo, front and back covers, page 3
Bonna Rouse: page 10 (bottom)
Robert Thomas: pages 8 (bottom), 17, 21, 24 (top), 25 (bottom right), 26
Tiffany Wybouw: pages 5 (middle), 6, 13, 14-15, 19, and all small humpback
    illustrations except where otherwise indicated

Crabtree Publishing Company

www.crabtreebooks.com   1-800-387-7650

PMB 16A
350 Fifth Avenue
Suite 3308
New York, NY
10118

612 Welland Avenue
St. Catharines
Ontario
Canada
L2M 5V6

73 Lime Walk
Headington
Oxford
OX3 7AD
United Kingdom

Cataloging in Publication Data
Kalman, Bobbie
    The life cycle of a whale / Bobbie Kalman & Karuna Thal.
    p. cm. -- (The life cycle)
    Includes index.
    Describes the physical characteristics, behavior, and migration patterns of humpback whales and their growth from calves to adults. The book also talks about the many dangers facing whales.
    ISBN 0-7787-0653-2 (RLB) -- ISBN 0-7787-0683-4 (pbk.)
    1. Humpback whale--Life cycles--Juvenile literature. [1. Humpback whale. 2. Whales. 3. Endangered species.] I. Thal, Karuna. II. Title.
QL737.C424 K35 2002
599.5'25--dc21
                                        2001047105

Contents

 # What is a whale?

Dolphins are toothed whales.

Whales may look like fish, but they are large **marine mammals** that belong to the order *Cetacea*. Marine mammals live in the ocean. Like all mammals, **cetaceans** are warm-blooded. Their bodies stay the same temperature no matter how warm or cold their surroundings are. There are two groups of cetaceans—*Odontocetes*, which are **toothed whales**, and *Mysticetes*, which are **baleen whales**. The largest whales in the world are baleen whales.

Humpback whales are baleen whales. You can see how huge they are by comparing the size of this humpback to the size of the diver swimming near its chin.

Baleen whales

Right whales, humpback whales, and blue whales are all baleen whales. Instead of teeth, these whales have baleen plates that hang from the tops of their mouths. Baleen is made of the same material as that of your fingernails. It looks like a comb with frayed ends. The frayed ends catch food.

baleen →

right whale

pleats

humpback whale

Thousands of tiny krill get trapped in the hairlike fringes of baleen.

A huge gulp!

A baleen whale takes in food by filling its mouth with ocean water. Pleats in its throat expand to hold the water. The whale then uses its tongue to push water out of its mouth. Any small fish and krill that were in the water get caught in the baleen. The whale swallows this food whole.

krill

Humpback whales sometimes make bubbles that surround and trap their prey like a huge net.

A whale sends out a great "whoosh" of air and water droplets as it exhales. Its spout can be seen from far away.

The magnificent humpback

Humpback whales are the fifth largest whales. Adult females are between 45 and 50 feet (13.7 - 15.2 m) long. Males are between 40 and 48 feet (12.2 - 14.6 m) long. The bodies of humpbacks and other whales are **streamlined**. They are round and narrower at both ends to allow these mammals to glide easily through water.

Very little is known about humpbacks and other large whales. Whales are difficult to study because they live in the depths of the world's oceans, and they are constantly on the move. Most of the information about humpbacks comes from people who observe them. Scientists use this information to learn how whales behave.

blowhole crest

blowholes

Humpbacks and other baleen whales have two blowholes that they open to take in air.

*(left) A **blowhole crest** is a raised area in front of the blowholes that keeps out water when the whale inhales.*

What is its real name?

The humpback's common name comes from the way it swims. Its **humped**, or arched, back lifts out of the water, as shown in the picture below. Its **scientific**, or Latin, name is *Megaptera novaeangliae*, which means "long-winged New Englander." Humpbacks have the longest **pectoral fins**, or flippers, of any whale—up to 15 feet (4.6 m) long. The fins look like underwater wings.

"Kohola" is the Hawaiian name for humpbacks. Many humpbacks spend their winters in Hawaiian waters.

 # What is a life cycle?

All animals go through a set of changes called a **life cycle**. They are born or hatch from eggs and then grow and change into adults. As adults, they **mate** and make babies. This book is about the life cycle of humpback whales.

Born underwater

Humpbacks and other whale babies **gestate**, or grow inside their mothers, until they are ready to be born. The babies, called **calves**, are **born live** underwater. They grow quickly and become adults in four to eight years.

A journey called migration

The life cycle of a humpback includes a long journey called **migration**. For part of the year, humpbacks live in **arctic**, or very cold, waters. They migrate to **tropical**, or warm, waters each winter.

Why do they migrate?

Adult humpbacks have a thick layer of fat, called **blubber**, under their skin. Blubber keeps whales warm in cold waters, but newborn calves have very little blubber. If they were born in icy waters, they would freeze! Humpbacks migrate so their babies can be born in warm waters.

A life span

A **life span** is the length of time an animal lives. Scientists are not sure how long humpbacks live. Humpbacks may have a life span of 30 to 40 years.

Humpback calves are born in tropical waters near places such as Mexico and Hawaii.

The great migrations

Humpbacks live in every ocean, but they are found in different areas at different times of the year. They migrate up to 7,000 miles (11 265 km) each year! In summer, they live in cold waters near the North or South Poles, where they feed. In autumn, they travel to tropical **breeding grounds** to have their babies. In spring, they return to the **feeding grounds** again. Look at the map below to see the yearly migration routes taken by humpback whales.

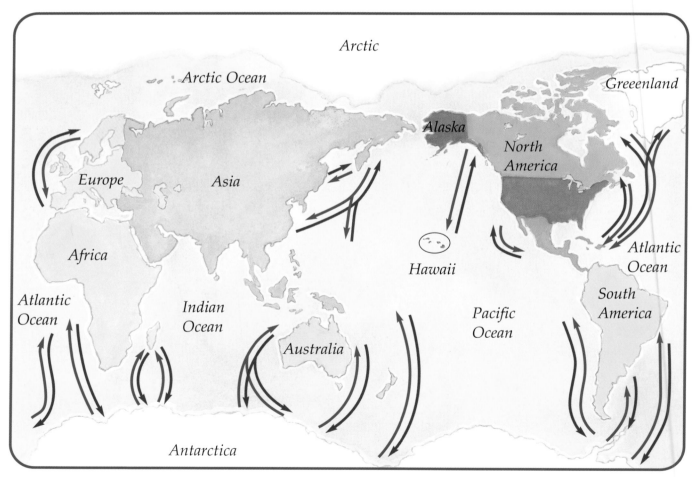

The red arrows show migration routes to the breeding grounds. The blue arrows show routes to the feeding grounds. Northern humpbacks travel south to the breeding grounds, and southern humpbacks travel north.

How do they know the way?

Scientists think that humpbacks follow cues in the environment to guide their travels. Ocean currents, changes in water temperatures, and the position of the stars may direct whales migrating to and from their breeding grounds.

Built-in compasses

Humpbacks have a substance called **magnetite** in their brains. Magnetite acts as a compass that helps these whales sense changes in the earth's **magnetic field**. It allows them to sense the direction in which they need to swim.

A calf is born

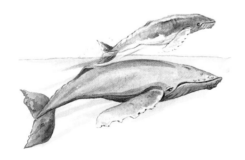

The calf in the photograph above is about two days old. Calves are pale gray when they are born.

Every winter, male and female humpbacks mate at the breeding grounds. A year later, the females give birth to their calves in the same waters. No one has ever seen a humpback birth. In captivity, baby dolphins are born tail first, so scientists believe that other cetaceans may also be born this way. Whale mothers give birth every two to three years, but sometimes they give birth only a year after their last calf was born.

A safe spot

To give birth, a humpback mother selects a spot near shore that is away from boats, sharks, and male humpbacks. The water must be shallow so that the baby can reach the surface to breathe air as soon as it is born. After the calf is born, mother and baby stay close to shore and rest for about a week.

The size of a flipper

At birth, the calf weighs over 3000 pounds (1364 kg) and is about the size of one of its mother's pectoral fins. Its color is much lighter than that of its mother.

Humpback mothers help their young calves take a breath of air by lifting them above the water.

Nursing and growing

Humpbacks and other whales usually give birth to one calf at a time. The newborn calf begins to **nurse**, or drink milk from its mother's body, soon after it is born. The mother's **mammary glands** make milk for the calf. The mother whale uses her strong muscles to squirt the milk into her calf's mouth. The calf nurses only as long as it can hold its breath, which is about three minutes. It nurses about forty times a day.

Whale milk

A calf drinks between 100 and 150 gallons (about 400 to 600 liters) of milk every day! Whale milk has twice the **protein** of cow's milk, and it is very thick. The milk you drink may contain one or two percent fat, but whale milk is fifty percent fat! It needs to be rich so that the baby can grow quickly and gain blubber before its journey to the feeding grounds.

15

Close to Mom

A humpback calf stays very close to its mother. Unless it is nursing, the calf swims just above her. In this position, it can ride on her head or back or hang onto her using one of its flippers. (See picture on page 9.)

Young calves need to breathe every few minutes, but their mothers can hold their breath much longer. The calves must swim to the surface alone for a breath of air. They then swim quickly back to their mothers.

Humpback mothers protect their calves from predators such as orcas and sharks. When a predator tries to attack a calf, the mother responds by thrashing her flukes, slapping her fins, and rolling her body. After nursing, this calf swims between its mother's protective pectoral fins.

This calf is getting a "piggy-back ride" from its mother.

17

The growing calf

The calf grows one foot (0.3 m) each month and develops a thick layer of blubber. By the time the mother and calf are ready to leave the breeding grounds, the calf is half its mother's size and weighs about 10 tons (9 metric tons). It has a lot to learn before it starts its long journey!

This humpback calf is leaping out of the water in a magnificent breach.

Swimming and breathing

As it grows, a humpback calf practices swimming to get ready for its first long trip. It also starts making deeper dives with its mother. To make a deep dive, the calf needs to practice holding its breath for longer periods of time. Its mother can stay underwater for up to twenty minutes without taking a breath!

spyhopping

Playing adult games

Humpback calves love to splash, leap, and dive. They **spyhop**, or stick their heads out of the water, to look around above the surface. They also learn to **breach** as they breathe. To breach, they thrust their bodies out of the water and fall onto their backs. The play of the calves helps them become strong swimmers and prepares them for adult life.

Its first long trip

At the end of winter, the calf is ready to make its first migration to the feeding grounds. It is still nursing, so it swims close to its mother. The other humpbacks are also getting ready for the trip. They start their journeys at different times.

The first to leave the breeding grounds are the newly pregnant cows, followed by the **juveniles**, or young whales that have left their mothers. Next are the other adults. Mothers with calves stay the longest at the breeding grounds to give the calves plenty of time to grow.

Weaning the calf

During the first summer in the feeding grounds, the young calf continues to nurse, but it also starts eating krill. The calf is **weaned**, or switched completely from milk to adult food, between six and eight months of age.

Immature whales

Once a young whale is weaned, it can leave its mother. The whale is no longer a calf. It is now an **immature**, or juvenile, whale. An immature whale is not yet ready to mate.

Playing with other whales

As the young humpback grows, it plays with other juveniles. The playful contests of the juveniles become serious competitions when the young whales grow into adults.

Ready to mate

It can take four to eight years for a juvenile humpback whale to become an adult. Once it is fully grown, the whale is ready to make babies of its own. It travels to the breeding grounds to mate.

To the breeding grounds

The length of time it takes to swim from the feeding grounds to the breeding grounds depends on where the whales live and how quickly they swim. It can take from two weeks to three months.

Humpbacks do not eat during much of their migration. They live off their blubber for up to eight months of the year. A female that gives birth loses as much as half her body weight.

Some scientists think that whales are able to rest half of their brain and use the other half to keep swimming. Dolphins are able to do so, but no one knows for certain whether whales also rest this way.

Who arrives first?

Mothers with their **yearlings**, or year-old calves, are the first to arrive at the breeding grounds. Next are the juvenile whales that are not yet **mature**, or adult. They are followed by adult males and females. The last to arrive are the female whales that are ready to give birth. These females stayed at the feeding grounds as long as they could in order to gain as much fat as possible before giving birth.

Competing to mate

At the breeding grounds, a humpback female with a calf is often accompanied by an **escort**. In the past, people thought the escort was a female that helped a mother take care of her calf, but scientists no longer believe this to be true. They now think that the escort is a male that stays with a cow to mate with her and to stop her from mating with other males.

"Stay away from my mate!"

Humpback whales perform some magnificent displays, such as those shown here. Scientist believe the males may perform these displays to compete for mates. When two or more males want to mate with a cow, they threaten each other other by singing, blowing streams of bubbles, and breaching. The competing males may then move on to more threatening behaviors such as slapping their heads or tails against the water or butting heads. The male that does not back down becomes the female's escort. He swims below the mother and calf, as shown on the opposite page.

head slap

tail throw

head butt

breach

The songs they sing

Male humpbacks sing long, complex songs made up of high chirps and cries and low moans, groans, roars, and snores. The humpback is the only whale known to sing these songs, which are repeated often, for several hours at a time.

No one knows how these whales make their sounds because they have no vocal cords. Scientists think that the whales sing by circulating air through the chambers and tubes of their **respiratory systems**, but no air escapes, and their mouths do not move.

Haunting songs

A humpback song is made up of sounds arranged in special patterns. The patterns create two to nine separate **themes** that are sung in a specific order. The themes last about 15 minutes and are then repeated. The complete songs are about an hour long.

Making up the songs

The songs do not change during the feeding months, but the singers make up new themes each year at the breeding grounds. They eliminate old themes and add new parts, so their songs are quite different at the end of a mating season than they were at the start. After a few years, the songs are completely new.

Different dialects

Each humpback **population** has its own song. The singers sing their own **dialect**, or version, of that song. Whales in the same areas sing similar dialects. Those that live in different areas or oceans sing different songs.

Only the males sing

Although females make sounds, only the males sing complex songs. People have heard whales singing mostly in the breeding areas, but males have also been recorded singing during migration.

Why do they sing?

Singing may advertise the fitness and willingness of a male whale to mate. Males may sing to attract females, but scientists believe that the songs are more like threats made to other males. Whales that are competing to mate use the songs to keep track of one another.

Singing for supper

Humpbacks also use a type of song to trap their food. People have heard groups of humpbacks making high-pitched noises in their feeding grounds. They use these "songs" to frighten fish into tight circles. When fish are in a group, the whales can catch them more easily.

Dangers to whales

Humpback whales are an **endangered species**, or a species that is in danger of dying out. If there are no members of an animal species left in the world, the species is **extinct**. Today, there are only 15,000 to 20,000 humpbacks left. This number is higher than it was a few years ago, but there are still many threats to humpbacks and other whales.

Whaling yesterday and today

People have been **whaling**, or hunting whales, for thousands of years. In the past, whaling was more difficult than it is today. Many whales were killed, but they were not overhunted. More recently, as ships and weapons became more powerful, some types of whales were hunted nearly to extinction. Whale populations around the world were severely reduced until the International Whaling Commission banned all **commercial** whaling, or whaling for business, in 1986. Some people, however, break the law and continue to hunt whales.

A few countries believe that the ban on hunting certain whales should be lifted, but scientists believe that the ban is still necessary to protect whales.

Noise pollution

Whales are very sensitive to sound. One of the newer threats to whales is noise pollution. Strange or loud sounds in the water confuse whales and can cause them severe harm.

Dangerous sounds

Sonar is used to locate objects under water. Sonar equipment sends out pulses of sound. These **sound waves** bounce off objects and return to the equipment. The length of time it takes for the waves to return measures how far away the object is. New kinds of sonar, such as Low Frequency Active Sonar (LFAS), are very loud and extremely dangerous to whales and all cetaceans. During tests of LFAS, dead whales with ear, lung, and brain damage washed up on shorelines.

Writing letters

There is plenty that you can do to help whales! You can take part in letter-writing campaigns to stop dangerous practices that hurt whales, such as using LFAS. Letting government officials know how you feel is an important way to bring about changes.

Get involved!

Did you know that the efforts of children helped free Keiko, the orca that starred in the movie *Free Willy*? You can get involved in efforts to help all kinds of whales.

Get connected!

There are many excellent websites that will keep you up to date on the latest news about whales. Many sites also have great tips about what you can do to help. Visit these sites for more information:

www.geocities.com/tokitae
www.pacificwhale.org/children
www.whaling.com
www.oceanfutures.org
www.ifaw.org

(above) Many whales get caught in fishing nets. This stranded gray whale tried to free itself from a fishing net and died on the beach.

For the love of whales

Watching the whale-watchers

Whales have been on Earth much longer than humans have. Can you imagine a world without them? It would be a sad place indeed! Seeing a whale is one of the most exciting experiences imaginable! Whales also seem to enjoy watching people. They often approach whale-watching boats to catch a glimpse of the people who are watching them.

Grateful for whales!

Find out everything you can about whales. Then write a list of reasons why you are grateful for whales.

A whale of a picture!

Imagine a safe and happy future for whales. Draw pictures of humpbacks singing and dolphins dancing in clean oceans that are free of noise and whalers! Hang your works of art where others can see them to remind people to think of whales.

Whale music

Have you ever heard a humpback sing? Ask your librarian or teacher to help you find tapes or CDs of humpback songs. Write a song that you think the whales might be singing to one another.

Amazing whales!

On a recent trip to Hawaii, my co-author Karuna, a friend named Ginny Walden, and I went on a whale-watching trip. We were disappointed because, after several hours, we still had not encountered any whales. The boat captain lowered a **hydrophone** into the water so that we could listen to the humpbacks sing, even if we could not see them. On hearing the beautiful humpback songs, we were inspired to sing to the whales whose songs we heard. Ginny taught us a song called Amazing Whales. We sang it to the tune of Amazing Grace. Just minutes after we started singing the song, three whales appeared out of nowhere and swam behind our boat. They then dove under it and came up a short distance ahead. Before they swam away, they waved their flukes at us, as if to say "Great song!" Amazing whales!

Amazing whales
We see your tails
Above the shining sea.
We send you love and healing, too.
We are your family!

Glossary

born live Describing a baby animal that is not hatched from an egg but emerges live from its mother

breeding grounds Warm ocean waters where whales mate and have calves

cetacean A group of marine mammals, including whales, that have nearly hairless bodies, wide front flippers, and flat tails

endangered Describing an animal species that is in danger of dying out

feeding grounds Cold ocean waters where whales live and feed

hydrophone An instrument used for listening to underwater sounds

juvenile Young; not yet an adult

magnetic field The electric current that pulls towards the poles of the earth

magnetite A mineral found in the brains of some animals that helps them find direction

mammary gland An organ in a female mammal that produces milk for her young

mate (v) To join together to make babies; (n) a mating partner

migrate To travel long distances in search of food or better weather

population A group of individuals living together in a particular place

protein A substance necessary for growth that is found in the cells of living things

respiratory system The system in the body that is used for breathing

species Within a larger group of animals, a smaller group with similar bodies and habits; for example, humpbacks are a species of whale

theme The main melody in a piece of music

Index

1 2 3 4 5 6 7 8 9 0 Printed in the U.S.A. 1 0 9 8 7 6 5 4 3 2